Everything You Need to Know About

School can be tough for students with dyslexia, but people are beginning to understand that it is a medical condition and not laziness or slowness.

Everything You Need to Know About Dyslexia

Meish Goldish

The Rosen Publishing Group, Inc.
New York

Published in 1998, 2001 by The Rosen Publishing Group, Inc.
29 East 21st Street, New York, NY 10010

Revised Edition 2001

Library of Congress Cataloging-in-Publication Data

Goldish, Meish.
Everything you need to know about dyslexia/Meish Goldish—
1st ed.
p. cm. — (The need to know library)
Includes bibliographical references (p.) and index.
Summary: Explains the causes and symptoms of dyslexia and discusses how to overcome this disability and become a good reader and writer.
ISBN 0-8239-3462-4
1. Dyslexia—juvenile literature. 2. Dyslexic children—Services for juvenile literature. 3. Dyslexic children—Education—juvenile literature [1. Dyslexia.] I. Title. II. Series.
LB1050.5.G645 1997
371.91'44—dc21
            97-11686
                CIP
                 AC

Manufactured in the United States of America

Contents

Introduction

One of the first things we learn as school children is how to read. Reading is a key that can unlock an unlimited number of doors. Storybooks invite us to visit imagined worlds. In magazines, we can read about fashion, politics, or music. Newspapers inform us of events happening across the globe or around the corner.

Often without thinking about it, we rely on reading to manage our daily lives and ensure our safety. We read labels on cereal boxes and soup cans to find out the ingredients. We consult the telephone book to locate a business or find the phone number of a neighbor. We read traffic signs. We read warning labels.

But what if a child has trouble learning to read?

Over 100 years ago, in November of 1896, a doctor in Sussex, England, published the first description of a learning disability that would come to be known as dyslexia. W. Pringle Morgan wrote in the *British Medical Journal*, "Percy F, aged 14, has always been a bright and intelligent boy, quick at games, and in no way inferior to others of his age. His great difficulty has been—and is now—his inability to learn to read."

Morgan describes a mystery that has stumped doctors, teachers, and parents for over a century. Why do some very bright people have trouble learning to read? People often assume that if someone is smart and works hard in school, he or she should have no trouble learning to read. But the experience of millions of dyslexics like Percy F has shown this assumption to be false.

Dyslexia is a language disability. It is also considered a learning disability. It affects a person's ability to read, write, and spell in accepted ways. Dyslexia tends to affect the ability to communicate in more subtle ways, too. For instance, someone with dyslexia may be pretty sure they know another person's name, but when they say the name, it comes out all wrong. Or, no matter how much a student with dyslexia studies for a test, the next day he or she might completely forget the material. Although just as smart as the other kids

Those who suffer from dyslexia often have other talents, such as musical ability.

in his or her class, it may take a student with dyslexia five times longer to do homework.

As much as dyslexics have a learning and language disability, they also have gifts. As we learn more and more about how the mind receives and digests information, we also learn that everyone's mind does not work in exactly the same way. While dyslexics may find it hard to express themselves in words sometimes, they may have a talent for thinking in terms of three-dimensional pictures. They may have a gift for music or art. They could be phenomenal gymnasts or great scientists and inventors. They may be very sensitive to the emotions of others. They may be highly perceptive about other people's thoughts and feelings.

Many people do not realize that they have dyslexia. Unfortunately, teachers and parents do not always notice that a child has a language disability. Often they find other explanations for a student's school troubles. Fortunately, if dyslexia is diagnosed, it can be managed. People with dyslexia can and do learn!

Chapter 1

Caleb

Caleb didn't like school very much. He hated most of his classes. English and social studies were the worst. They required lots of reading, and Caleb didn't like to read. He wasn't good at it. He also wasn't very good at math or science. The only class he really enjoyed was shop, where he made things with his hands. Shop was fun, and he was good at it. Best of all, it required no reading.

Caleb had no friends in school. He had known most of his classmates since kindergarten, but he wasn't close to any of them. Some kids teased Caleb for being a poor student. As a result, Caleb stayed away from everyone. He became a loner.

In class, Caleb was always quiet. He prayed that teachers wouldn't call on him. He couldn't answer their questions because he never did the reading homework the night before.

Caleb also skipped most of the writing assignments. When teachers asked why, he always made up an excuse.

Some teachers felt sorry for Caleb. They came to expect less from him than from other students.

But some teachers scolded Caleb for being lazy. They told him he wasn't trying hard enough. They urged him to work harder. They warned that he might flunk his classes.

Even so, Caleb always managed to pass. Most times, his grades were just above failing. Some teachers passed him out of pity. He was a poor student, but he never acted up or caused trouble, so most teachers ended up giving him Ds.

In truth, Caleb really was smart. And he was trying hard in school. His real problem was something that nobody—not even Caleb—realized.

The Trouble Begins

Caleb's problems started in first grade. That's when he first felt that he was different from his classmates. Other kids found it easy to learn. They could spell and read and do math. It was fun for them. But Caleb wasn't able to do those things.

He had trouble looking at letters and words. He didn't see them the way other children did. When Caleb saw the letter "b," it looked like a "d." When he saw a "p," it looked like a "q." The letters seemed to flip and jump around the page.

Letters were only one problem. Soon the teacher was writing whole words on the board. She wrote the word "saw," but to Caleb it looked like "was." The word "mop" looked like "nob." "Now" looked like "new." The letters kept moving and jumping around.

Reading aloud was very hard for Caleb. His teacher would point to a word and say it aloud. Caleb would look at the word and repeat it. But when he saw the same word later, he couldn't remember how to say it. He wasn't sure how to sound out the letters.

Caleb found it hard to write letters and words. He often made letters backwards. Instead of writing "c," he'd write a backward "c." Instead of "s," he'd write a backward "s."

Caleb did poorly on spelling tests. As the teacher said each word, Caleb listened for its sounds. But he wasn't sure which letter made which sound. So his spelling was often wrong.

Those with dyslexia sometimes perceive letters as being written backwards.

Caleb also had trouble seeing numbers. Like letters, they seemed to flip around. The number "12" looked like "21." If Caleb tried to write "35," it came out "53."

Even Caleb's speech was poor. Sometimes he forgot words he wanted to use. Once he meant to tell his teacher that he had lost his book. Instead he said, "I can't find, you know, the thing we read from."

Caleb's first-grade teacher was very concerned. She thought Caleb was not paying attention. She told him he had to work harder. Caleb felt that he couldn't. He began thinking that he was stupid.

Some days the teacher spent extra time with Caleb after school. He practiced writing letters and words. But despite his efforts, his writing was still poor.

The teacher spoke with Caleb's parents. She said that Caleb wasn't trying hard enough. That surprised his parents. At home, he was never a problem. Sometimes he had trouble following directions, but his parents couldn't see why Caleb would be lazy in class.

Caleb's parents spoke with him. He wanted to tell them about his reading problems but he was confused and ashamed. He didn't want them to know that he was different. So instead, he promised to try harder in class.

Caleb's parents tried to help him at home. They coached him in writing and math. Sometimes Caleb's father would get angry. He'd yell, "Caleb, pay attention! You're not trying!" Caleb knew it wasn't true. It made him cry.

Finally, his parents decided that Caleb needed to be in a special class in school. There was a class for students thought to be slow learners. But Caleb became very upset when his parents mentioned it. He didn't want to be different from his classmates. He refused to go.

Things Get Worse

Caleb barely passed first grade. In second grade, he hoped that his problems would go away. Instead, they grew worse. The teacher gave harder spelling words and more writing assignments. The books were harder to read, too.

Caleb ran into a new problem: following the teacher's instructions. Caleb did okay when the directions were short: "Open your spelling book to lesson six."

But when the directions were longer, Caleb got confused: "Open your spelling book to lesson six. Take out a pencil and paper. Write your name at the top. Number the paper from one to ten." Suddenly Caleb was lost. He couldn't remember anything. He couldn't do what the teacher had asked.

Caleb tried to hide his problem. He looked around to see what other kids were doing and copied them. But that made the teacher angry. She said he was cheating.

Over time, Caleb found ways to cope with his problems. In reading groups, Caleb figured out ahead of time which passage would be his. While waiting for his turn, he looked over the passage. He went over the words he knew. When it was his turn to read aloud, he paused at strange words. Usually, his teacher filled them in for him.

Sometimes Caleb asked his older sister to do his homework for him. She did it because she loved him and felt sorry for him.

Every year Caleb hoped his reading problems would go away, but they never did. He still had a hard time following along in class. Yet he often fooled his teachers. He always looked straight ahead, as if he was paying attention. Really, Caleb's mind was a thousand miles away. He only got caught if the teacher asked him a question.

A New School

In sixth grade, Caleb entered middle school. A teacher there was concerned about his work. She had Caleb tested. His scores were low. Caleb was put in a class for students labled "slow learners." He didn't want to be there. Other kids called him and his classmates mean names. But this time, he couldn't get out of attending the class.

In class, Caleb got special help. Sometimes he had the teacher's time all to himself. They worked on reading, writing, and math. Caleb tried. But the extra help still didn't erase his problems.

Insecure people sometimes put down those who are different to make themselves feel superior.

Caleb stayed in the special class through the eighth grade. He wanted to quit school and get a full-time job after that, but his parents wouldn't let him. They told him he had to keep trying.

A Big Surprise

In ninth grade, Caleb entered high school. He went back to regular classes. But all his learning problems remained. The only good part of Caleb's day was shop class, where he designed and made things with his hands.

Then, something happened that changed everything for Caleb. The local art museum held a contest. Students were asked to create a sculpture. The winning entry would be displayed at the museum.

To everyone's surprise, Caleb won. His sculpture was made of different metals. It had large circles, triangles, and rectangles. It looked impressive. The local newspaper ran a picture of Caleb with his work of art.

Caleb was asked to speak about his work at a school assembly. Again he surprised everyone. His speech was excellent. He had memorized what he wanted to say, so he didn't need to read anything.

Caleb received many compliments on his artwork and speech. He surprised his classmates and teachers.

Caleb's English teacher was puzzled. She saw that he could do good work and speak well. It was clear that he was neither slow nor lazy.

The teacher had Caleb tested again. This time she used a special test. The results proved what she had suspected. The test revealed Caleb's real problem: He had dyslexia.

Chapter 2

What Is Dyslexia?

Dyslexia is a language and learning disability. The term was coined by Rudolf Berlin of Stuttgart, Germany, in 1887 to describe the inability to read. Dys means "difficult." Lexia means "word" or "language." Dyslexia is a condition that makes it hard for a person to read words and use language.

There are many forms of dyslexia. You can have one or more forms. A person with any form of dyslexia is called a dyslexic.

Originally, dyslexia only meant problems in reading. But later, people began to use the word for problems in other areas, such as spelling, writing, and math. The severity of dyslexia can range from minor problems with spelling to complete illiteracy.

Today, not all experts agree on what dyslexia is. They define it in different ways. They have different ideas about what causes it. They even disagree on how to treat it. But they do agree on one thing. Dyslexics are not stupid. Most have average intelligence. Many are above average. With the right help, all dyslexics can overcome their learning problems.

Who Is Dyslexic?

The exact number of dyslexics is not known. Some experts think that as many as one out of every fifteen Americans is dyslexic. Government statistics indicate that 25 million Americans, or one out of every ten, are functionally illiterate (can't read or write). The primary cause of their illiteracy is dyslexia; over 85 percent of adult illiterates are dyslexic. It is further estimated that 10 to 15 percent of school-age children have dyslexia. Yet despite the large numbers of people with dyslexia, it is estimated that only 5 percent of dyslexics are ever properly diagnosed and given appropriate help.

Until recently, nothing was known of dyslexia. Dyslexics got little help. In school, they were put in classes with developmentally disabled students. As adults, they were given only simple jobs because they were often illiterate. It was very difficult for dyslexics to become successful, independent, productive members of their community. Few people recognized

Until recently, dyslexics were often assigned menial jobs because they were illiterate and mistakenly thought to be "slow" or unintelligent.

that dyslexics were enormously talented and gifted in some areas and could do much to enrich society.

What Causes Dyslexia?

No one is sure what causes dyslexia. Experts have many theories. Here are a few:

◎ **Theory 1: Difficulty processing language. More specifically known as the Phonological Model, this theory argues that dyslexia stems from the brain having difficulty breaking words down into language units called phonemes. For example, the word "cat" consists of three phonemes: "kuh," "aah," and "tuh." In fact, different combinations of just forty-four phonemes produce every word in the English language.**

◎ **Theory 2: Poor hearing. Dyslexics may have hearing problems that keep them from sounding out letters. These problems may have begun with an ear infection in childhood.**

◎ **Theory 3: Injured nervous system. The body's nervous system allows signals to travel to the brain. A dyslexic's nervous system may have been injured at birth** or it may have been damaged by a high fever or a concussion. As a result, the brain doesn't receive signals the right way.

◎ Theory 4: Genetics. Dyslexia may be passed from parent to child. Experts have found that many dyslexics have a dyslexic parent, so dyslexia may be in one's genes. It may be inherited at birth.

◎ Theory 5: Viral disease. Pregnant women can be exposed to flu or other viruses. Sometimes a virus can be passed on to the fetus. A virus can damage the paths by which brain cells travel in the fetus. Normal brain development is affected.

◎ Theory 6: Multiple causes. Dyslexia may have many causes, not just one. That would explain why there are many different forms of dyslexia. Each form may be the result of a unique combination of factors that have affected a person.

◎ Theory 7: Neurological problems. The lower centers of the brain don't work properly so that signals from the inner ear or eyes to the brain get scrambled (making reading and listening, for example, very difficult). As a result, the brain misinterprets the information it receives from the eyes and ears. This is why letters and numbers are often flipped or words waver, jump, or bunch up on the page.

◉ Theory 8: Is the student necessarily the problem? It may seem more efficient to teach all students how to read in one particular way or using one particular method. But what if class sizes were smaller and teachers had more time to provide students with individual attention? Perhaps, they then might be able to address the different learning styles of their students.

Myths About Dyslexia

Even though we do not yet know exactly what causes dyslexia, we do know what it is not. It is not acting up, carelessness, or laziness. It is not an emotional problem. It is also not caused by poor eyesight and is not a sign of low intelligence. Below are some of the most common myths about dyslexia.

Myth: Dyslexia Is the Result of Poor Vision

As recently as the 1920s, experts thought that dyslexia might be caused by a problem with one's eyesight. Experts recommended eye training and strenghtening, often with the use of eye patches. Although the cause of dyslexia is still unknown, most current research suggests that it is a language rather than a vision disorder.

Myth: More Boys Than Girls Are Dyslexic

Boys' reading disabilities are identified more often than girls', but studies indicate that this identification is biased. Research shows that dyslexia affects boys and girls equally. Unfortunately, dyslexia is generally under-diagnosed, and even more so in the case of girls.

Myth: People Outgrow Dyslexia

Researchers who monitored dyslexics from first through twelfth grade found that the disability persists into adulthood. Even though many dyslexics learn to read accurately, they continue to read slowly and not always with the greatest of ease.

Myth: Dyslexics Are Not Smart

Intelligence is in no way related to dyslexia. There are scores of brilliant and accomplished dyslexics—among them the poet William Butler Yeats, General George Patton, the writer John Irving, and Wall Street investor Charles Schwab.

Forms of Dyslexia

A dyslexic can have many reading problems. Dyslexics often reverse letters, so that "p" looks like "q." They may see words backward and read "pan" as "nap." They can mix up letters, seeing "m" as "n" or "u" as "w." The word "of" may look like "off," "on," or "or." Sometimes, they see entirely new words. A dyslexic might read the sentence "Once there was a pig" as "Once there was a hen."

When someone reads aloud, dyslexics have a hard time following along. When dyslexics read aloud, they stumble over words and say them incorrectly. They may say "animal" as "aminal." They may read a word correctly on one page, but later, they won't recognize the same word.

Some dyslexics can read words well, but they don't understand what they're reading. They must read a sentence several times to get its meaning. They may understand an idea easily if it is told to them. But reading the same idea is hard. Some dyslexics can both read well and understand what they read, but find it very hard to write or spell.

Difficulty with writing or spelling (sometimes called dysgraphia) is a very common problem for dyslexics. They often see words as jumbles of letters. Dyslexics can't picture a word in their minds. They may spell it correctly out loud but still spell it wrong on paper. They may mix up letters or leave some out. They may write "stand" as "stad," or "coffee" as "coffb."

Many dyslexics have trouble paying attention. Their minds tend to wander. They can't focus on reading or other tasks for very long. This problem is called attention deficit disorder, or ADD. Some dyslexics are also hyperactive, or restless. Some dyslexics have ADD combined with hyperactivity, a condition known as attention deficit hyperactivity disorder (ADHD). One person with dyslexia and ADD describes it as "Running daydreams—a process of always rapidly creating in your mind, so you never hear what others really say, or you forget what they say. Therefore you can't hear or see things around you accurately."

Dyslexia affects many areas of life. Dyslexics may have trouble dialing a telephone number. They may not be able to follow directions. If told to turn left, they may turn right. If asked to mail a letter, they may get distracted and forget to do it. Dyslexics can be disorganized. They often can't remember where they put things. Dyslexia can also cause a person to be clumsy.

As you can see, dyslexia can cause many problems. As a result, dyslexics sometimes have low self-esteem or consider themselves stupid. Some become quiet and withdrawn; they hope people won't notice them. Other dyslexics react differently: In school, they are the class clown; they hope that joking around will make them popular and hide their real problems.

Dyslexia can cause so many different problems that dyslexics may develop low self-esteem.

Are You Dyslexic?

Only a test given by an expert can show if you are dyslexic. But there are signs to watch for. Do any of these statements describe you?

Reading:

- I see letters and words in reverse.
- I see letters and words bunched together.
- I see letters grow and shrink.
- I see letters move and disappear.
- I see words that aren't there.

- I have trouble sounding out letters.
- I make many mistakes when reading aloud.
- I often skip words or lines.
- I often lose my place on the page.
- I can read only one word at a time.
- I feel dizzy or get headaches while reading.
- I don't understand what I read.

Writing and Spelling:

- I reverse letters when writing.
- I bunch letters together.
- I mix up or leave out letters in words.
- I have very poor handwriting.
- I have a hard time copying words.
- I can't picture words in my mind.

Math:

- I have trouble with addition and subtraction.
- The numbers seem to jump around.
- I come up with a different answer than everyone else does when I do multiplication or division.

- I don't see some of the problems on the page.
- I add when I should subtract.
- I divide when I should add two numbers.

Speaking and Listening:

- I can't remember words I want to say.
- I have a difficult time making some speech sounds.
- I don't hear or listen to what is said to me.
- I have a hard time remembering instructions.
- Sounds seem closer or farther away than they really are.

Other Signs:

- I often confuse left and right.
- I have trouble telling time and being on time for appointments.
- I am not well organized.
- I have trouble making decisions.
- My mind wanders easily.
- It's hard for me to sit still.

◎ I feel dumb.

◎ Other kids seem to learn and understand things much faster and read with much less difficulty.

◎ Someone in my family has dyslexia.

If you find yourself agreeing with many of these statements, especially in the reading, writing, and spelling categories, you may have dyslexia or another learning disability. Speak with your parents or with a teacher or counselor about being tested for dyslexia.

Chapter 3

Coping with Dyslexia

Dyslexics cope with their problems in different ways. Some ways are good, but others only mask the problem. These are sometimes called compulsive solutions. They may help a dyslexic for the moment, but they do not help in the long run. In fact, they often make the problems worse, in that people do not receive the support they need.

Here are some compulsive solutions that many dyslexics rely on.

Reading Pictures

Jason can't read words well. So he "reads pictures" instead. In school, he figures out a story by looking at the pictures. When shopping for a

birthday card, he looks for a picture of a cake on the cover. In restaurants, he orders from food pictures on the menu.

But reading pictures doesn't always work for Jason. Some books have few pictures. Some menus have no pictures. Once Jason bought a birthday card for his girlfriend. It had a pretty cake on the cover. But Jason was embarrassed later. The card he bought turned out to be for an anniversary.

Memorizing

Miguel has trouble taking notes so he relies on his memory to get by. In school he tapes his classes. Later, he reviews the tapes. He memorizes everything on them. On tests he writes what he remembers from the tapes.

For Miguel, memorizing often works. But not always. Once he got sick and missed school for two weeks. He was too embarrassed to ask a friend to tape his classes. He couldn't catch up later. He ended up with poor grades for that term.

Using Others

Anthony is dyslexic, but he doesn't tell his friends. Instead, he uses them to get by. In school, he takes the same classes that they do. They study together, so Anthony learns the material. Some friends even write papers for him. He lets them play his computer games in return.

Making Jokes

Tong uses humor to hide his dyslexia. He figures, "If I make a joke, it will take the pressure off. No one will notice that I can't read."

Tong has become the class clown. When asked to read, he makes funny faces and gestures. The class always cracks up. Even some teachers laugh. But others do not. Tong's attempts to be funny often get him into trouble.

Causing Trouble

Some dyslexics want to get into trouble. That's the case with Benton. In class, he is sometimes asked to read aloud or write on the board. Instead, he talks back to his teacher. That lands him in the principal's office. Benton is pleased by that. It gets him out of class, so no one can make fun of him.

Of course, getting kicked out of class doesn't really help Benton. It makes him fall further behind. Sometimes he is suspended from school. And he never gets help for his reading problems. Instead, teachers think he has emotional problems.

Due to frustration, dyslexics sometimes act out and can get into trouble.

Treatments for Dyslexia

As you can see, compulsive solutions do not really help dyslexics. For years doctors have sought a cure for dyslexia. So far, they have not found one. But they have found ways to help dyslexics to cope. No treatment works for everyone. But each treatment has helped a number of individuals.

The following are some of the treatments now offered.

Ear Medication

Some dyslexics take antihistamines and drugs for motion sickness. That's because their doctors think dyslexia comes from a disorder in the inner ear. The disorder speeds up signals that go to the brain. As a result, the eye sees things too quickly. It's like trying to read a sign from a speeding car. Letters are blurred, scrambled, and reversed. The medicines slow down the signals that go to the brain, so reading becomes easier.

Chiropractic

Chiropractic is a system of therapy which treats disease by trying to improve nerve function. Some doctors think that dyslexia is caused by a bone problem. They say this bone problem keeps the eye muscles from working freely. As treatment, chiropractors massage the skull bones that affect the eye muscles. They also work to improve the dyslexic's posture when reading. They believe that eye reflexes start at the base of the spine, so sitting properly can help one to see correctly.

Megavitamins

Other doctors believe that dyslexia may be caused by a chemical disorder in the brain. They treat the disorder with megavitamins or megaminerals. These are much higher dosages than the usual amounts of the vitamin or mineral. Doctors believe that this treatment sets the brain's chemistry at normal levels. Once that happens, according to this theory, the dyslexic has less trouble reading.

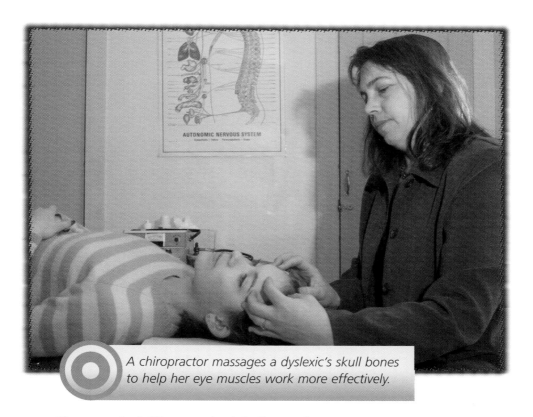
A chiropractor massages a dyslexic's skull bones to help her eye muscles work more effectively.

Essential Fatty Acid Supplements

Some nutritionists think that dyslexia is caused by a deficiency in essential fatty acids (EFA), a necessary nutrient for the proper functioning of the eyes, brain synapses, and nerve tissues. Some people sell a nutritional supplement that includes tuna fish oil and other oils rich in fatty acids and Vitamin E.

Special Diets

Some dyslexics are hyperactive. Sugar adds to their energy, so their doctors put them on diets that lower their intake of sugar. Other doctors recommend not eating wheat or milk products, because they often contain sugar. Others say to avoid foods with artificial flavoring, such as soft drinks.

Tinted Lenses

Recently, the use of lenses or page overlays tinted with color (such as blue or red) have been shown to be helpful to some dyslexics. Some dyslexics seem to be very light sensitive; their brains can't properly filter out certain kinds of light, making reading difficult. Black letters on a white page look like they are jumping. Tinted lenses or overlays screen out the light for dyslexics, making the letters stand still.

Exercise

Some research indicates that regular exercise seems to boost a dyslexic's concentration, memory, and overall performance in school.

All the treatments mentioned so far are controversial; experts do not agree whether they really work. Some are too new for their results and benefits to be clear yet. Each treatment seems to work for some dyslexics, but not for all.

Multisensory Treatment

Today, the most widely accepted treatment for dyslexia is a multisensory approach. It combines the senses of sight, sound, and touch. The dyslexic learns how words sound and how they look on paper. The student also learns how the mouth moves to form the words and how the hand muscles move when the words are written.

The multisensory approach involves special exercises that help a dyslexic learn. If you are dyslexic, here are some things you might do:

- Say the sound of each letter in the alphabet. Notice how your mouth, lips, and tongue move to make the sound.

- Listen over and over to letter sounds on tape. Then repeat the sounds yourself.

- Say each sound in a word as you trace its letters with your finger.

- Read a word on a flash card. Then look at a picture next to it that represents the word.

- Listen to a book on tape while following the text.

- Use a white card to block out everything but the sentence you are reading. It can help keep you from being distracted.

- Read a paragraph the first time for the main idea. Read it again for the details.

◎ Write your own story. Then read it aloud.

◎ Plan a daily or weekly schedule with the help of a calendar. Get used to organizing your time each day.

◎ Break down instructions into separate steps. Then follow the steps one at a time. Ask your teachers to help you break down their instructions on paper.

Classroom Strategies

◎ Sit up front and close to the instructor so you can get help whenever you need it.

◎ Do not sit near a window.

◎ Keep an assignment book or appointment book with you so you don't forget important due dates, events, or meetings.

◎ Ask your teacher for an outline of each day's lesson plan.

◎ Use an expanding file folder, instead of loose individual folders, to keep hand-outs/papers/homework organized.

◎ Use erasable pens for writing assignments.

When Taking Notes:

◎ Divide your paper in half and write "topics" on the left side and "details" on the right side.

◎ Create note cards by using index cards. Have a heading and then write the details below.

◎ Write down all unfamiliar or difficult words in bold print on note cards and also write the definition.

◎ Review several note cards daily.

◎ Ask your teachers for help when you need it.

◎ Enroll in a keyboard or typing class; some dyslexics find it easier to take notes and jot down their thoughts using a computer rather than pen and paper.

Chapter

4

Family Matters

If you have dyslexia, your family can be a very important source of help. They can help you cope with your problems. They can help you with exercises to make reading easier. They can offer patience and understanding. They can give emotional support.

Yet a family can also make things harder. Some families don't understand the problem of dyslexia. Some refuse to accept it. Others don't know how to help.

Realizing the Problem

Often, parents don't realize why a child can't read. In all other ways, the child may be normal. Everyone else in the family reads well. There are no problems at home. So why is the teacher saying there are problems in class?

You may feel like your parents blame you for your learning problems. If you're dyslexic, your parents may think you are not trying. That may be what your teacher has told them. Your parents become angry and they tell you to stop being lazy. They may even punish you.

Other parents feel guilty and blame themselves. They think they somehow caused the problem and feel frustrated because the problem won't go away. It becomes a vicious cycle of blame, guilt, and frustration.

Parents may blame the child and themselves if they don't realize that their child is dyslexic. They first have to recognize the real problem.

If you have a reading problem, your parents need to know why, and so do you. The first thing to do is to get tested. You and your parents can ask your school to arrange this.

Discovering Hidden Talents

Our son Dennis was diagnosed with dyslexia and ADD when he was in third grade. While he had difficulty sitting still and learning to read, write, and spell, he was blessed. Like other people with learning differences, his brain had pockets of amazing creativity, energy, insightfulness, and determination. Once we understood what was going on in his head and realized that he was not "slow," we figured out all sorts of ways to cope with his learning and attention problems. He developed a passion for playing music. Now he plays fourteen instruments! After attending college, he built a career performing and selling his music. Dennis still can't sit still and rarely reads for pleasure. However, his hard work, energy, and creativity have added up to a great life!

Homework

Homework can be a huge challenge for dyslexics. Family members may be tempted to do the work for you, but that will not help you learn.

There are more useful things your family can do to help if you're dyslexic. For example:

◎ **Set aside a specific time each night for doing your homework. Your family can make sure that you have the quiet you need to do your work.**

◎ **Tell your parents exactly when each assignment is due. Also, try to explain what each assignment is about.**

◎ **If you have trouble getting started, tell your parents. They may have some good suggestions. Talk about it together. But do the reading or writing yourself.**

◎ Study together with family members for quizzes and tests.

When Studying on Your Own

◎ Write everything down: your class assignments, extracurricular activities, daily chores.

◎ If you are a visual person, use pictures, graphs, charts, or diagrams.

◎ Create a soothing study environment: make sure the room is quiet and there are no distractions; play soft, quiet music; unplug the phone and turn the television off; take notes while you're reading.

◎ Organize a study group before an exam or study with a partner.

◎ When handling a long, complex assignment, break your work into small chunks, take frequent, but brief, breaks, stretch your legs, get something to drink, etc.

◎ Prioritize your time: Do the assignments you like the least first!

Studying with a group of friends can make learning easier for dyslexics.

The more exposure you have to your assigned topics, the more likely you are to learn them: read illustrated books about the topics; listen to information on tape; see films about the topics; talk to people who are experts in the topic areas; go to historical societies and art, science, or natural-history museums for information.

Developing Self-Esteem

Many dyslexics have a hard time liking themselves. They see themselves as different from everybody else. They can't read or write well. They can't keep up in class. Other people may tease them. They feel that they can't succeed. They see themselves as failures.

Dyslexics often have low self-esteem. Sometimes that makes family matters worse. If you're dyslexic, you may not cooperate if you feel sad or angry. You may think, "What's the use? Nothing I do is good enough anyway!"

Family members can help to change that. They should try to boost your confidence. You are not doomed to failure. You can learn to cope with your problems, and you can succeed. But your family may need to remind you of that at times.

Here are some ways to help improve your self-esteem:

Know Your Strengths and Weaknesses:

◎ **Pursue your strengths. If you're a gifted artist, take art classes. If you're a great athlete, join a team. If you're great with people, volunteer or get a job at a school or hospital.**

◎ **Get help in your areas of weakness (from teachers, friends, professionals).**

◎ **Find out more about dyslexia so that you can gain the perspective you need to understand your difficulties and be able to explain them to others.**

You can improve your self-esteem by spending time with people who enjoy your company.

Speak to a Couselor or Therapist if:

◎ You find that your feelings of sadness or anger get in the way of work and fun.

◎ You have difficulty sleeping or sleep more than usual.

◎ You lose your appetite or eat more than usual.

Chapter 5

The "Gift" of Dyslexia

Many experts consider dyslexia a kind of gift. That's because dyslexics often see things in a different way than the average person sees them. Since they can't read well, dyslexics rely on reasoning skills more than other people do. They may look at a problem and find a solution that others miss. Their level of curiosity is often greater. They think in pictures instead of in words. They use all their senses to understand things. They have vivid imaginations. If you're dyslexic, you can harness these special talents and do great work.

Famous People with Dyslexia and Related Learning Problems

Many dyslexics lead very successful lives. Some have even achieved greatness.

Leonardo da Vinci (1452–1519) was a brilliant painter who also studied anatomy, astronomy, botany, and geology. He designed many machines and drew plans for hundreds of inventions.

Galileo (1564–1642) was a remarkable astronomer. As a child, he had a talent for building toys. During Galileo's lifetime, many people disagreed with his scientific research which showed that the Earth revolves around the Sun and not the other way around. The Catholic Church even put him on trial and punished him for his discoveries! But he was later proven correct.

Ludwig van Beethoven (1770–1827) was one of the greatest classical composers of all time. But as a young boy he was hard to get along with. He often fought with his father and his brothers. One of his music teachers said Beethoven would never compose music. Why? Because he couldn't follow instructions!

Thomas Edison (1847–1931) was an ingenious and prolific inventor, yet his teachers called him slow and uncreative. He left school at an early age. His mother taught him at home instead. In addition to being dyslexic, Edison was also deaf for most of his life.

Albert Einstein (1879–1955) was a brilliant scientist, yet he did not speak until the age of four. He could not read until the age of seven. He failed classes and dropped out of high school. Yet he became one of the world's greatest mathematicians.

Many famous celebrities, such as Tom Cruise and Cher, suffer from dyslexia, but it hasn't kept them from having successful careers.

Agatha Christie (1890–1976) was a famous writer who had dyslexia. She wrote eighty-three books of detective and mystery stories, and sixteen plays.

Cher (b. 1946) is a successful actress and singer. Until the age of eighteen, she was unable to read. She didn't find out that she had dyslexia until she was thirty. Yet she still managed to become a popular television and movie star, and she won an Academy Award (the Oscar) for acting.

Whoopi Goldberg (b. 1955) is a popular movie actress and comedienne, yet she had to cope with many challenges before achieving success. School was hard for her. Besides being dyslexic, she was also addicted to drugs.

Greg Louganis (b. 1960–) was only sixteen years old when he won a silver medal in swimming in the 1976 Olympics. He also won gold medals for diving in the 1984 and 1988 Olympics.

Carl Lewis (b. 1961–) is an Olympic athlete. In the 1984 summer games, he won four gold medals for track and field. He also won medals in the 1988, 1992, and 1996 games.

Tom Cruise (b. 1962–) is one of Hollywood's highest-paid actors. His box-office hits include *Top Gun*, *Rain Man*, *Mission: Impossible*, and *Jerry Maguire*.

Other famous and successful dyslexics include: Michelangelo, Sir Isaac Newton (who proved that gravity exists), Alexander Graham Bell (inventor of the telephone), Harrison Ford, Danny Glover, Jay Leno, River Phoenix, Robin Williams, Pablo Picasso, Muhammad Ali, Magic Johnson, Walt Disney, John Lennon, John F. Kennedy, and George Washington. So if you are dyslexic, you're in very good company!

Accept Yourself

Don't think about how fast others are progressing. Don't compare yourself to others who may win awards or get better grades. Just think about your own achievements. Remember that it is not your fault that your mind works differently. Above all, try not to become discouraged. Ask your teachers, parents, and friends for support.

Chapter 6

Getting Help

A dyslexic is not a problem child: He or she is a child with a problem. Too often, we think that dyslexics are lazy, uncaring, and maybe even unintelligent. Our misunderstanding makes these people lose confidence in themselves and in their abilities. In this chapter you will learn about trained professionals who work with dyslexics, helping to clear up these hurtful misunderstandings and to unlock dyslexics' potential.

Get Testing

Before anything else, you must find out if you are dyslexic. You can do that by taking a test. You can ask to be tested in school. Your teacher can tell you whom you should speak to about it. Or you can go to a private clinic in your town or city. Look in the yellow pages of your local telephone book. There may be clinics listed under Reading Improvement Instruction or Reading Clinics. If not, look in the back of this book under Where to Go for Help. Call one of the organizations listed and ask where the nearest clinic is. The type of people who are qualified to test for dyslexia include clinical and educational psychologists, school psychologists, learning disability specialists, and medical doctors with experience in diagnosing learning problems. If you are found to be dyslexic, you can start to get help immediately. If you're not dyslexic, ask the testing people where you should go for the reading help you need.

It's the Law

All public schools are required by law to provide learning disability testing and special help for dyslexics. The Individuals with Disabilities Education Act, passed in 1975 and reauthorized in 1990, guarantees free public education for all disabled students, including dyslexics. Many schools have special programs set up for dyslexic students. Usually, the students work in small groups. They receive instruction from trained teachers, reading specialists, and tutors. They work on reading, writing, spelling, and math. Some schools work with private clinics, tutors, or college programs. The students travel off campus each day for their instruction.

Professional Help

There are many professionals who help dyslexic students. Some work within schools. Others work in their own offices and see students privately.

- School psychologists are trained to diagnose learning problems, including dyslexia. They also know about tutoring programs that are available outside of school. They consult with teachers and offer counseling to students.

- Clinical psychologists work with dyslexic students who have serious social and behavioral problems in school.

- Diagnosticians are experts who try to identify the specific learning problems of each dyslexic student.

- Physical therapists treat physical problems that a dyslexic may have. These include disorders of muscles, bones, and nerves.

- Psychiatrists deal with special problems that a dyslexic may have. The problems include attention deficit disorder (ADD) and hyperactivity.

◉ Social workers work with dyslexics and
their families. They help them cope with
problems that arise at home.

◉ Occupational therapists focus on job
training skills for dyslexic students.

If you're dyslexic, you may not need the help of all
the types of professionals mentioned here. Each
dyslexic has different needs. But it is good to know
that many types of professionals are available.

Public Agencies

Dyslexics who are not students can also get help.
Many government agencies provide assistance. If you
are not in school, call one of these agencies. You can
find their numbers in the telephone book. They
include the State Department of Education, the State
Developmental Disabilities Office, and the State
Vocational Rehabilitation Agency.

Special Schools

Some schools have special programs for people with
dyslexia. They include the Gow School in South Wales,
New York; The Winston School in Dallas, Texas; the
Eagle School in Greenwich, Connecticut; and The
Greenwood School in Putney, Vermont.

Most special schools for dyslexics are private, not public. They may be expensive. But many of the services they provide are also offered in public schools, for free! So check around for programs in nearby public schools before signing up for a private school.

Help Yourself

Many people can help you cope with dyslexia. But no one can help until you first decide to help yourself. If you have a reading problem, don't deny it. Don't pretend it will go away by itself. Instead, accept that you need help. Start by getting yourself tested.

If you have dyslexia, you can deal with it. It is a challenge, but one that can be handled successfully.

So if dyslexia is making you feel discouraged, remember that with continued effort, success is right around the corner. Thomas Edison, the inventor of the electric light bulb and a famous dyslexic, made about 1,000 light bulbs before creating one that actually worked. A reporter once asked him how it felt to fail 1,000 times. Edison replied, "I didn't fail 1,000 times. The light bulb was an invention with 1,000 steps."

Glossary

antihistamines   Drugs that relieve suffering from
   allergies by shrinking the blood vessels.
attention deficit disorder (ADD)   A condition
   in which a person is unable to pay attention for
   very long.
chiropractic   The practice of treating illnesses or
   disorders by pressing and moving the spine and
   joints of the body with the hands.
compulsive solutions   Ways of solving a problem that a person uses over and over, even
   though they may not be helpful in the long run.
contagious   Spread by contact.
disability   A condition that leaves one unable to
   move, act, or work in a normal way.

disorder A condition that prevents a part of the body from working in its normal way.

genetics The study of how people pass on traits to their biological children.

hyperactive Extremely restless; unable to sit still for even a short period of time.

megavitamins Also megaminerals. Special vitamins taken in large doses to regulate chemical reactions in the body.

multisensory approach A program for coping with dyslexia that involves the senses of sight, sound, and touch in the reading process.

nervous system All the nerve cells and nerve tissues in the body, including the brain.

self-esteem How you think of yourself, your sense of self-worth.

theory An idea that explains how or why something happens, without complete proof.

word blindness Another term for dyslexia; the inability to read words, despite good vision and normal intelligence.

Where to Go for Help

In the United States
AVKO Dyslexia Research Foundation
3084 West Willard Road, Suite W
Clio, MI 48420-7801
(810) 686-9283
e-mail: AVKOemail@aol.com
Web site: http://www.avko.org

Dyslexia Research Institute
5746 Centerville Road
Tallahassee, FL 32308
(850) 893-2216
e-mail: dri@dyslexia-add.org
Web site: http://www.dyslexia-add.org

The International Dyslexia Association
8600 LaSalle Road

Chester Building, Suite 382
Baltimore, MD 21286-2044
(800) ABC-D123 (222-3123)
(410) 296-0232
e-mail: info@interdys.org
Web site: http://www.interdys.org

Learning Disabilities Association of America
4156 Library Road
Pittsburgh, PA 15234-1349
(412) 341-1515
e-mail: ldanatl@usaor.net
Web site: http://www.ldanatl.org

National Center for Learning Disabilities
381 Park Avenue South, Suite 1401
New York, NY 10016
(212) 545-7510
Web site: http://www.ncld.org

In Canada
Learning Disabilities Association of Canada
323 Chapel Street, Suite 200
Ottawa, ON K1N 7Z2
(613) 238-5721
e-mail: information@ldac-taac.ca
Web site: http://www.ldac-taac.ca

For Further Reading

Barrie, Barbara. *Adam Zigzag.* New York: Laureleaf, 1996.

Betancourt, Jeanne. *My Name Is Brain Brian.* Topeka, KS: Econo-Clad, 1999.

Davis, Ronald D. *The Gift of Dyslexia: Why Some of the Smartest People Can't Read and How They Can Learn.* New York: Perigree, 1997.

Janover, Caroline. *Josh: A Boy with Dyslexia.* Burlington, VT: Waterfront Books, 1988.

Simpson, Eileen B. *Reversals: A Personal Account of Victory Over Dyslexia.* Rev. ed. New York: Noonday Press, 1998.

Smith, Joan M. *You Don't Have Time to Be Dyslexic.* Sacramento, CA: Learning Time Products, 1996.

Index

About the Author

Meish Goldish is the author of more than thirty fiction and non-fiction books for children and young adults. A former high school English teacher, he visits many elementary and high school classrooms annually to talk about writing. He is an avid theatergoer who also performs his own one-man musical show. He currently lives in Teaneck, NJ.

Thanks to Barbara Berman and the students of John Adams Middle School in Edison, NJ.

Photo Credits

Cover, pp. 2, 8, 13, 17, 28, 35, 46 by Antonio Mari; p. 21 © Telegraph Colour Library/FPG; p. 37 by Cindy Reiman; p. 48 © Kathy McLaughlin/Imageworks; p. 51 (Tom Cruise) © Robert Hepler/The Everett Collection; p. 51 (Cher) © The Everett Collection.

Design and Layout

Thomas Forget